Contents

Introduction

Adding people to your painting adds another dimension. Putting people in the picture helps with perspective, creates atmosphere and reality. Imagine Trafalgar Square with no people in it, the scene would be lifeless and unreal.

To create the energy, and the feeling that I am part of the scene I am painting, I use paint in a loose impressionist style. People are included with the minimum of brush marks, but care is taken with the tones. These must be correct to create the 3D effect. Detail is unimportant. You can recognise a person from just a few tonal blobs, because of the person's stance. Several people have said that they recognise someone in one of my paintings from just a few brush marks!

When I first started painting I was interested mainly in buildings and scenery, but once those first people were included, adding people became addictive, and from that point on I started looking at the interaction between people; drinking coffee and chatting, a busking band on the street, a child playing on the beach. The energy and movement they inspire becomes the main focal point, so I loosen up the background even more. Just as you would view a scene, concentrating on a band or a couple in a restaurant, you remain aware that there are more people around, or buildings, windows, etc. That's how I try to translate the scene. Using strong tones and sunlight help to enhance the composition and create a strong image.

You will find subject matter in all sorts of unexpected places, just be ready and observant. Always choose a subject you are inspired by, then the rest will be easy.

African Dancer
Just a few minimal brush strokes create the energy and vibrancy of this African dancer. A few small, brightly-coloured brush marks around the dancer suggest the heat of the day.
Size: 8" x 10"

Opposite
Exmouth Donkeys
The sand is kept pale and the donkeys and children are painted in strong paint for contrast. The distant buildings are painted in pale washes and very loosely.
Size: 9" x 11"

PEOPLE AREN'T SCARY (REALLY)

A guide to painting people

Marilyn Allis

First published in Great Britain 2007 by The Minster Press, Wimborne.

This new, enlarged edition published September 2008 by Tabella Publishing LLP, 6 Winterborne Monkton, Dorchester, Dorset, DT2 9PT, info@tabella.co.uk
www.tabella.co.uk

tabella

ISBN 978-09558088-2-1

Photographs and design by Marilyn Allis, Mill Lane Gallery, 9 Mill Lane, Wimborne, Dorset BH21 1LN.
T: 01202 880084
E: marilyn.allis@btopenworld.com
W: www.marilynallis.co.uk

Previous page:
Rouen in the rain
Although not a sunny day, the strong tonal contrasts of the light hitting the wet pavement, along with the bright colours of the umbrellas, create an atmospheric painting.

Below:
Pigeons and Florentinos
People engaged in activity make for a compelling composition.

Materials & Equipment

You can start painting in water colours with a small amount of materials and equipment, introducing a few more colours as you gain in confidence. The smallest amount of space is needed.

Paints

I use all SAA water colour paints. Always use Artist quality, it is cheaper in the long run, as the pigments are stronger and less chalky. The colours I mainly use are: Sepia, Burnt Umber, Raw Sienna, Lemon Yellow, Cadmium Yellow, Light Red, Cadmium Red, Alizarin Red, Cobalt Blue, Ultra Marine Blue, Prussian Blue and Intense Violet.

Paper

To help create movement and an impressionistic painting, a rough paper is essential. It gives you lots of help in creating dry brush marks, but washes work equally well. A thinner, 90lb paper stretched gives a much brighter painting than using a heavy paper. Arche rough 90lb, Fabriano rough 90lb and Saunders Waterford rough 90lb are all highly recommended.

Palette

A kidney-shaped palette with deep wells works excellently. I use mine continuously, just rinsing under a warm tap before I start painting again. If I don't paint for a while and the paint has dried up, I just add more paint from the tubes, this gets worked in, no paint is ever wasted doing this. Deep wells are essential, because you need to pick up plenty of pigment on your brush, which will give you strong vibrant colours. If you squeeze out tiny amounts of paint, you will add a lot of water and the colour you first put onto your paper will dry very pale and insipid. The colour disappears before your eyes. Use a ceramic rose for mixing large quantities of wash.

Brushes

I use only three brushes, this is all you need. The SAA Whopper, SAA size 16 and the SAA All Rounder. The Whopper is a very large synthetic brush with a fantastic point, ideal for putting on large washes quickly, but painting around anything that needs to be kept clear. The SAA All Rounder and SAA size 16 are smaller brushes and ideal for general painting.

Hairdryer

On the whole it is better to leave water colour washes to granulate, but as washes need to be completely dry before applying dry brush marks, a hairdryer helps to speed up this process.

Pencils & Eraser

I tend to use a 2B or 4B pencil and I draw quite strongly. As I paint very quickly and need the tones to be accurate, a strong drawing means I can see easily were I am going. I like to rub out my pencil marks after the painting has dried. I use a putty eraser for this, it removes only the pencil marks and not the paper's surface.

Useful Colour Mixes

Skin Tones – Light red with a tiny bit of Sepia added. White skin when painted is a much darker tone than you expect.

Shadows – Intense Violet makes an interesting shadow. Grey can be very boring.
Large shadow areas can be broken up by using an unmixed mixture of French Ultra Marine and Burnt Umber. Vary from brown to blue to break up large areas.

Blonde Hair – Raw Sienna for where the light hits the hair and Sepia for where the shadows fall.

Sand Mix – Add a tiny bit of Sepia into Raw Sienna. Make this very watered down, almost like a watermark.

English Sky – Cobalt Blue with a hint of Light Red *(the red just takes off the edge of the bright blue)*.
French Ultra Marine mixed with a tiny amount of Burnt Umber. This makes a slightly stronger sky.

Mediterranean Sky – Phthalo Blue on its own is fantastic for giving that feeling of heat and colour.

Trees – Prussian Blue mixed with Sepia and a hint of Cadmium Yellow. This works very well for the dark darks of an English tree. When these pigments are used the greens look very natural.

Donkeys – Burnt Umber with a hint of French Ultra Marine. Raw Sienna mixed with Cobalt Blue, and Sepia on its own. Donkeys come in a great range of colours, and integrating these mixes will help you differentiate between the animals.

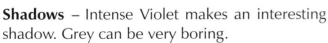

Techniques

1. Dry Brush Marks

Dry brush marks are created by painting using the side of the brush, filled with a thick mixture of paint, run the brush on its side along the bumps on a rough paper.

2. You can create a finer version using a credit card edge. Put thick paint on the edge of the card and run over the bumps of the paper.

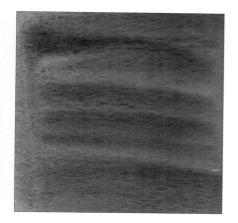

Granulation

This makes large areas look more interesting as the pigments build up in the bumps of rough paper. Some mixtures of paint don't granulate very well. Burnt Umber mixed with French Ultra Marine granulates really well. Once you have applied the wash let it dry naturally. If you use a hairdryer it will stop the paint granulating at the point you dry the paint.

Wash

This is the term used for applying large areas of water colour. Usually as a background.

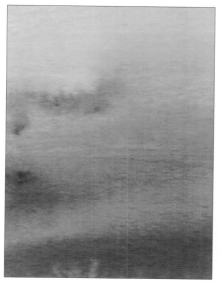

Granulated Wash

Pigment is added to initial wash to create a build up of colour.

Damp next to Damp

I use this a lot for buildings, animals and clothes. The colours blend and merge slightly, so you have a softer painting. If the paint dries the result can end up looking a little like painting by numbers.

1

MARRAKECH
USING COLOUR

The heat was extreme in Marrakech. The bustle of people, motorbikes weaving in and out of the tiny back streets, was truly manic. Warmer colours are needed to depict this scene, not the palette we would use for English summer paintings. Raw Siennas, Light Reds, Alizarin Crimsons for buildings, with Phthalo Blue for the sky will help create this hot market. I have taken a lot of time with the drawing, putting in a lot of detail. This will mean that I can paint fairly quickly with large washes, but still maintain the correct tones and create a looseness in the building structure. I have adapted the photograph I am using to make a better composition and to lose the people in the foreground as they would distract if included.

MATERIALS/COLOURS USED
Fabriano rough paper 90lb
SAA Water Colour Paints

Raw Sienna

Cadmium Yellow

Sepia

Alizarin Crimson

Cadmium Red

Cobalt Blue

Phthalo Blue

Prussian Blue

Intense Violet

1. Mix a small wash of Cobalt Blue for the distant part of the street. Whilst still very wet run into it a mix of Raw Sienna and a little Alizarin Crimson. The Cobalt Blue will give you recession in the street, pushing the background into the distance.

2. Paint the two people who are the main focal point first. I will use Cadmium Yellow for the man's robes, so he shows up more. Add a little Prussian Blue to the shadow areas of his clothes. Alizarin Crimson and Cadmium Red are used for his partner's robes, with Intense Violet for her shadow areas. Dry brush marks can be put in once dry to depict the creases in the fabric.

3. Put an Intense Violet wash over the shadow on the board to the right of the couple. The stripes are made up of a thick mixture of Alizarin Crimson. I have put some jagged lines over the symmetrical lines to break up the monotony of this area.

The buildings are very complex, so need to be broken down quite a bit. First, paint in any of the coloured shapes you can make out. This will help you place the tones of the buildings.

4. Gradually complete the background of the buildings, applying first well watered-down Raw Siennas and Alizarin Crimsons to the parts that the sun is hitting, then thicker mixes of Alizarin Crimson and Intense Violet for the shadowed areas. Concentrate more on the tones than the colours and apply very, very quickly.

5. Keep the left hand side light in tone, as this is where the sun is hitting, and the right hand side much darker in tone.

6. Make sure that any buildings in the far distance are kept blue; again, this will push them into the background. Do this, too, with the distant small figures. Painting

4

5

them on the blue side, will push them back into the distance.

7. Keep the bike very basic with a few very simple marks of Prussian Blue and Sepia.

You can now see how dark you can make the sky in tone. Paint that in Phthalo Blue.

Use the edge of a credit card to make any straight line marks on the buildings.

This technique gives a lovely broken straight line on a rough paper.

Add shadows using an Intense Violet mix. I felt the front needed something extra, so with artistic license paint a Phthalo Blue shadow. A few dabs of Phthalo Blue were added to the buildings. This was to balance the colours in the finished painting.

Size
36cm x 53cm
14" x 21"

MUSICIANS
USING COLOUR

MATERIALS/COLOURS USED

Paper: Leonardo Hahnemuhle 600g rough

These musicians are fantastic to watch and listen to. The energy they have is electric. I really want to reflect this in the finished painting. I have used a combination of photographs for reference and will exaggerate the movement. I will keep the colours warm and fairly strong. I do not wet the background first as this will help to keep the colours more vibrant. Also, I can leave a few white marks which will add sparkle. I have used a paper that I don't normally use as it has a smoother, harder surface, and will produce more movement in the washes.

Raw Sienna

Light Red

Burnt Sienna

Burnt Umber

Sepia

Cadmium Orange

Alizarin Crimson

French Ultra Marine

Prussian Blue

Cobalt Blue

White Gouache

1

If colours run slightly it all adds to the movement and energy. Leave the musical instruments for the moment as these need to be slightly more defined.

The two girl violinists can be painted using mainly Prussian Blue and Sepia, varying the mixes from black to blue. I will make the clothes of the girl standing behind slightly more blue. I will also give her a red T-shirt which will help to balance the colours in the finished painting.

1. Mix up several washes of colour ready to apply quickly. One of Raw Sienna, a Burnt Sienna and Cadmium Orange. Mix plenty as you don't want to run out half way through. Put these washes straight over the girl's trousers. The trousers will be dark and you can then use some dry brush marks.

Add some neat Cadmium Orange and Burnt Sienna into the top left hand corner and the bottom right hand corner. Put these in whilst the washes are still damp.

2. Dry really well before you paint in the figures. Use a Cobalt Blue wash for the guy's trousers and Alizarin Crimson for his shirt. The first washes can be well watered down for the parts of his clothes that the light is hitting. Use a thicker mixture of the same colours for the medium tones. Mix Light Red and Sepia for his skin tones, Prussian Blue and Sepia for his hair. Put next to skin whilst that paint is still damp.

3. Once completely dry. add dry brush marks to indicate creases in the fabric of the clothes. Squint and indicate any shapes that are very dark.

2

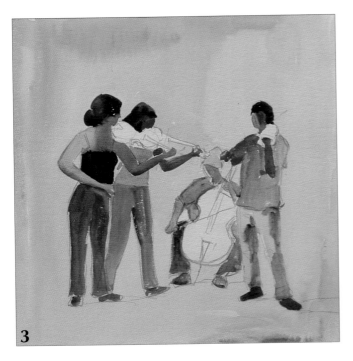

3

4

4. Use a Burnt Umber for instruments, so they are slightly different in colour to the skin tones. The two violins next to each other on the left hand side need to be separated, use Burnt Umber for the one in front and Cobalt Blue for the other. Use Sepia for the dark shadows on the instruments.

5. Rub a little White Gouache onto the side of a credit card and slide this along where you want the bows of the instruments. For the shadows I have used a French Ultra Marine.

At the moment it doesn't look too much like Covent Garden, and I really would like that to be more obvious. I will add one of the famous arches. Run some clear water over the whole area where the arch is to go. Then, with some Burnt Sienna, make an arch. One side merging into the clear water, the other as a dry brush mark.

6. I will also add a minimal amount of dry brush marks around the musicians to emphasise movement.

5

6

MOROCCAN BEACH

USING COLOUR

The bright sunlight hitting the beach and sea has such an appeal, causing silhouetted figures to look strong in the distance. The colours in reality are quite bland as the sun has bleached out any natural colour from the sand and sea. You can really use your imagination with the colours you use, to make a very vibrant colourful painting reflecting the heat and brightness you experienced on the beach. I will use a very basic palette of just four colours.

MATERIALS/COLOURS USED

Paper: Daler Rowney Rough Board

Raw Sienna ⟶

Light Red ⟶

Alizarin Crimson ⟶

Phthalo Blue ⟶

1. This drawing is very basic, just placing people were I want them. The washes need to be more clear and loose. Mix plenty of wash colours beforehand. Decide which colours you will use and where you are going to place them. Using the Whopper brush and clear water, wet the paper, leaving a band of white paper running through your composition. This will give a lovely brightness to the finished painting.

2. Use the Whopper brush to quickly place your washes onto the paper. First add the Phthalo Blue for the sky. Then, a mix of Alizarin Crimson and Phthalo Blue for the distant hills. Mix a little Alizarin Crimson with some Raw Sienna for the sand, also use a wash of Light Red. Remember to leave clear the band of white that runs diagonally through the painting. When you paint in your figures, this will give tremendous impact.

You have to be careful that the horizon line and the line of walking people aren't in the middle of your composition.

4. Make sure that your washes are completely dry before adding the figures. Let the background dry naturally, as natural granulation in the pigments of the paint will occur.

Mix a thick mixture of Phthalo Blue and Alizarin

Crimson for the silhouetted figures. Add a little Light Red for the limbs.

The shadows are the same mixes of colour as the figures, just mixed with slightly more water.

With a few simple brush marks and a minimal palette you have captured an atmospheric day on a Moroccan beach.

Size
35cm x 50cm
19" x14"

BIKERS
UNUSUAL COMPOSITIONS

This couple had such an interesting appeal, I couldn't resist painting them. I have drawn them in quite a lot of detail. The sunlight was extremely strong, which makes for a fantastic water colour painting; the shadows formed will help create a real three-dimensional painting. I decided to focus totally on the couple and leave most of the background white to create the impression of heat, and give more impact.

EQUIPMENT/MATERIALS
Paper: Rough surfaced
 90lb Fabriano
Colours: SAA Water Colour
 Paints

Raw Sienna

Cadmium Yellow

Light Red

Alizarin Crimson

Sepia

Cobalt Blue

Ultra Marine Blue

Prussian Blue

Phthalo Blue

Intense Violet

1. For the flesh I used a mix of Light Red, with a touch of Sepia. I will paint the girl first as she is the main focal point. Squint to find where your light shapes are and then look for your darker shapes. For the darker tones use a thicker mix of Light Red and Sepia. Add whilst the paint is still wet and it will blend in with a soft edge.

2. I will use Intense Violet for the shadow on the girl's white T-shirt (grey would be a bit colourless in the hot sunshine).

The brown skirt also looked a bit colourless, so I will change that to Alizarin Crimson. It will also make for a much better focal point. For the lightest area

1

of the skirt add plenty of water to the Alizarin Crimson and then bleed in a thicker mixture, (more paint, less water) whilst still wet for the medium tones. Mix Intense Violet with the Alizarin Crimson for the dark tones.

Your work must be completely dry before putting on dry brush marks of thick Intense Violet and Alizarin Crimson to show the folds in the cloth of the skirt. These marks are very satisfying as they bring the subject to life.

3. Use a wash of Raw Sienna for the girl's hair, with Sepia for the dark tones.

You have to be careful that some parts of your composition don't end up merging into each other; for example, the man's shirt, the girl's T-shirt and her handbag are all the same colour. To separate this on my painting, I will make the handbag yellow instead of white and the shadow on the man's shirt will be Cobalt Blue.

I will use Cadmium Yellow for the man's shorts, with Prussian Blue for the dark shadows.

Bald heads are easy.

Where the light is hitting the head, put a very watered wash of pale Cobalt Blue, blend in around it a mix of Light Red and Sepia.

4. Detail on the bike is difficult to see; don't worry about this, just squint and paint in the light shapes, using a mix of Cobalt Blue and Light Red, and fill around those with any darker shapes you can make out with Prussian Blue and Sepia.

The tyres are a mix of Cobalt Blue and Light Red, well watered down for where the sun is hits. Add a thicker mix for the shadow areas.

3

4

I think Phthalo Blue will work well for the artificial blueness of the bike. Mix in Prussian Blue for the dark tones.

For the shadow colour I will mix French Ultra Marine Blue and Alizarin Crimson.

To add colour to create the heat of the day, I will make light marks of Raw Sienna and Alizarin Crimson, and watered the edges to soften. Before you do this make sure that your painting is absolutely dry.

1

END OF AN ERA

CREATING MOVEMENT

MATERIALS/COLOURS USED

Paper: Rough surfaced 90lb Fabriano

Raw Sienna

Burnt Umber

Sepia

Cobalt Blue

French Ultra Marine

Prussian Blue

Cadmium Yellow

Lemon Yellow

Cadmium Orange

Cadmium Red

Light Red

Alizarin Crimson

Intense Violet

This scene captures magical memories from childhood. Wonderful hot summers spent on the beach, the crowded busy beach buzzing with people. I decided to leave as many people in this painting as I could, to create the atmosphere. To do this I had to focus on the main characters, and paint others very loosely and watery to give the impression of their presence, but not so they became too prominent. I have used artistic license and omitted the horrible concrete, and might well leave out the distant hills. I can decide this once I have painted in the people and donkeys.

1. Using lots of water mix Raw Sienna and Sepia. Make sure you mix enough mixture. You don't want to run out half way through. If the paint dries whilst you are mixing more, you can end up with blotches and 'cauliflowers'. This mixture should be almost like a water mark (just a hint of colour). Using a Whopper brush you can put the wash on very quickly running it straight over the donkey's legs, which are much darker, so dry brush marks will be used later, to put these in. Whilst the sand is still wet, drop in some Burnt Umber, and Raw Sienna. Do make sure the paint you are dropping in is of a thicker consistency. If you have too much water you will again create blotches and horrible marks. These extra paints dropped in will break up the sand area, and granulation will occur which will add interest.

2. Make sure the sand is completely dry before painting in the people and donkeys. The scene is quite complex, so

I will break it down. First, I will paint the main people who are a focal point, that will then help me to see where I am going with the painting.

A good mixture for skin tones is Light Red, with a touch of Sepia. The tones are usually much darker than you expect, and will create a strong contrast. If you are unsure, place a white piece of paper next to the skin tone on your reference material, you will be surprised at the darkness of the skin. Use a mix of Sepia and Prussian Blue for the hair. For the shorts of the girl, I will use Intense Violet, with a mix of Prussian Blue and Sepia for her top. I have applied the paints very quickly as I would like them to blend and merge, to create movement. I don't want them to look like 'painting by numbers'.

Once dry, add a few very minimal dry brush marks to the clothes. Use a very thick mixture of Intense Violet for the shorts.

4

5

3. Complete the four other main characters in the same way. I have altered some of the colours of the clothes to add more beach colours and vibrancy to the scene.

4. The crowds of people behind the main characters need to be softer, so they are painted paler and more loosely. You need to be aware they are there, but not too detailed.

5. The two central donkeys are the focal point, so these are painted first. French Ultra Marine mixed with Burnt Umber for one, and Cobalt Blue mixed with Raw Sienna for the other. The light part of the donkey's underneath is easy. Paint straight over the donkey and then with a clean brush wipe over the underneath and remove the pigment. Use dry brush marks for the donkey's legs. This helps to create the impression of movement.

The distant donkeys and figures must again be painted paler, with a watered down mixture of paint. Paint the blankets

Size
29cm x 51cm
11" x 20"

6

with Prussian Blue and Lemon Yellow, saddles a mixture of Ultra Marine and Burnt Umber. The bands on the donkey's heads are Alizarin Crimson.

6. Keep the sea and sky very simple. Looking at my figures, they are very colourful. I now need the background to be as simple as possible. I will apply a wash of French Ultra Marine mixed with Burnt Umber around the figures, washing it away to nothing, into the sky. Remember, sea is always the same colour as the sky, just a couple of tones darker.

A good shadow mix is Burnt Umber and Ultra Marine. Vary this thoughout your shadows so you don't end up with a big area of one colour grey. It can be bluer in places and browner in others. This all adds interest.

The sand needed a little interest so I have added a few brush marks of Burnt Umber and Ultra Marine, soften the edges with clear water. This will also enhance the 'holiday' feeling.

SPEEDWAY

CREATING MOVEMENT

MATERIALS/COLOURS USED

Fabriano Rough surfaced 90lb

Raw Sienna

Cadmium Yellow

Burnt Umber

Sepia

Light Red

Cadmium Red

Alizarin Crimson

Cerulean Blue

Cobalt Blue

French Ultra Marine

Prussian Blue

Intense Violet

The colour and energy found at motocross or speedway events is amazing. Even on a dull cloudy day, with no shadows, the movement and colour can still be captured. There is so much material on tap to be used.

I usually stand on a corner to take photographs, that way you catch the movement on the bends and this adds interest, with the various positions of the riders and bikes. The compositions also look better if they are grouped. Photographs at the beginning of a race mean the contestants are closer to each other. Later, they spread out, and the composition will not be so dynamic.

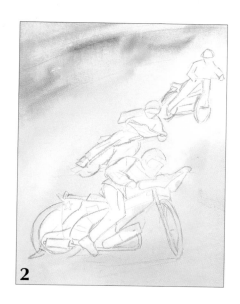

2

1. I will move the bikes slightly closer together to improve the composition. I think painting in the portrait will better give the feeling of cornering. It is difficult from the reference material to make out too much detail, I will draw in blocks of shapes that the tones and colours make. Don't worry when you can't make out all the details. Just look for shapes that you can see.

2. Apply light washes first onto wet paper. I will use a Raw Sienna with a hint of Alizarin Crimson, French Ultra Marine with Burnt Umber and Cadmium Yellow. I will apply the washes straight over the riders and parts of their bikes. Later I can use dry brush marks to add even more movement. For the barriers in the distance I will randomly drop in French Ultra Marine Blue and Alizarin Crimson. Spread the colour quickly in a directional line whilst wet, to give the impression of speed lines blurred in the distance.

3. Make sure the background is completely dry before you paint the main biker. You need to break this down as the

3

rider and bike can at first seem overwhelming. First, I will paint the rider. That way I can see where to proceed with the bike later. The skin tone is a mix of Sepia and Light Red. Only a little bit of flesh is showing under the rider's helmet. Paint in any white that is in shadow using Intense Violet. The helmet is Alizarin Crimson with Prussian Blue for the dark areas. Paint very quickly so that the paint merges slightly and adds to the movement. Where light is hitting the biker, use a brush with clear water to take out paint whilst wet, and give you your light tone.

4

4. In the same way pick out bike colours, using a Cobalt Blue and Light Red mixed together for the medium tones. Cerulean Blue for the main bike colour. With Prussian Blue and Sepia pick the dark areas out with dry brush marks.

The middle rider needs to be very loose, so he doesn't interfere with the main focal point. Wet him completely with clear water and drip in the colours that you see. The third rider can be put together very loosely, damp next to damp.

5. To balance the painting and add a little more colour, brush in, with the Whopper brush, some directional lines of the bend with Raw Sienna and Cobalt Blue.

Spray under the wheels with clear water from a spray bottle to create a little more movement and dust.

Size
34cm x 45cm
13" x18"

5

1

ST. MARK'S SQUARE
USING LIGHT

My daughter and I had been really looking forward to visiting Venice, we had only one day there and it poured with rain. At first I was really disappointed. I wanted to paint all the famous scenes that I had seen in paintings, only they were always in sunshine. However, I was so surprised that the light was so bright hitting the wet streets and the canals. Instead of strong shadows, I had brilliant tones and colour reflections. I actually ended up with a range of far more interesting and untypical paintings of Venice. The bright umbrellas were too good not to paint. In the end I was pleased that we did have rain all day. I was captivated at the way the group of people were trying to keep up with their guide and made for a slightly different foreground to St Mark's.

MATERIALS/COLOURS USED
Fabriano Rough surfaced 90lb

Cadmium Yellow

Burnt Umber

Sepia

Cadmium Orange

Alizarin Crimson

Light Red

Cadmium Red

Cobalt Blue

French Ultra Marine

Prussian Blue

Intense Violet

2

1. I will drawn this in great detail *(detail meaning light and dark shapes)*. I find it better to put a lot of detail in to start with, as this helps me to paint quickly and loosely. I will alter some of the walking stances of the people. They can look strange or awkward when painted if legs are too rigid.

2. I will need to paint St Mark's first, keeping it very pale and very loose. I want the viewer to be aware that this is St Mark's Square, but I want the figures to be the main focal point. I will use a well watered down Intense Violet and occasionally add Burnt Umber to vary the tones of the building. These will be the main colours throughout the painting. Painting very quickly, I will add a little Cobalt Blue for the building on the left.

3. The tower is very ugly and the redness of it dominates. Use artistic license and tone this right down, making it the same colour as the other buildings in the distance. Use the Whopper brush for large areas of wash and the All Rounder for more detailed work.

4. Using the distant St Mark's as a guide I am going to put a wash of Cobalt Blue and Burnt Umber mixed with Intense Violet over all the foreground. Then very quickly, whilst still damp, use a damp natural sponge to drag the pigment out of the areas that the light is hitting.

5. Make sure washes are completely dry before starting to paint the figures *(you want the figures to be crisp and you*

3

4

5

Sepia. Use lots of dry brush marks on the legs to create movement. The skin tones are a thick mix of Light Red and Sepia.

To make the marks of the umbrella handles, put your mix of Prussian Blue and Sepia along the edge of a credit card, then just run along the paper. The bumps in the paper pick up bits of the paint and you get some lovely broken straight lines.

want to be able to make dry brush marks). I will make a start with the brightly-coloured umbrellas, some are, in reality, black, but I have altered these to bright colours. With a brush that has just clear water on it, pull out the colour from the tops of the umbrellas where the light is hitting.

6. The figures are very silhouetted so mix thick washes of colour, some very dark areas can be Prussian Blue and

7. The distant figures can be painted very quickly. Just indicated with coloured blobs, very randomly painted, using blues, violets and red with hints of light red. These can mix and blend slightly, and this technique works very well for giving the impression of crowds in the distance.

6

7

The reflections are made from picking up on the colours you have used to paint the figures and putting them underneath the relevant people. You can add a little clear water in places to give that very wet day feel.

I can now see how much more needs to be added to the background of St Mark's. If I had done this earlier I probably would have put in too much and over-worked it. Just add a few darker tones and dry brush marks to complete the painting. I can now paint in the sky using Cobalt Blue with a hint of Light Red. Putting the sky in last means I can judge the correct tone it needs to be.

Size
35cm x 52cm
13" x 21"

BETHANY

TONE

MATERIALS/COLOURS USED
Arche Rough 90lb

Lamp Black ⎯⎯⎯⎯⎯⎯ ●

Cadmium Red ⎯⎯⎯⎯⎯ ●

Sometimes when you are looking for inspiration, it is good to look at exhibitions, and your imagination can be fired up once again. Tone is so important for the basis of whatever you paint, if you get it wrong the painting won't work. This is an excellent exercise in sorting out tones into just light and dark. Inspired by Andy Warhol, I took some photographs of my daughter. I tried to get sunlight on at least a third of her face, with some strong shadows on the rest. Once you have selected your photograph it may help to either photocopy it into black and white or turn it into a black and white photograph. This will give you a little extra help in looking at the different tones and understanding them.

Some of the tones are obvious. For the very lights

I will use the white of the paper, and the very darks the Lamp Black paint. It's the medium tones that are more tricky. You have to decide with a medium tone whether to make it white or black, so as to enhance the finished painting. Take some time to think it through. You

1

Light	Medium	Dark

2

a very thick mix of water colour paint, a lot of paint pigment and very little water. I want the colour to look almost like the screen prints, strong and not wishy washy in any way. I will add a little red to some areas of hat and neck to balance the colour in the finished painting.

Use a very thick mix of Lamp Black. Pick out the main shapes you see. Before your eyes an image that you recognise starts to emerge.

You can use any three colours to experiment with.

could even use several photocopies and shade in areas you think will work, before you actually start painting. This really gets you thinking and analysing tone.

The light tones I am keeping white *(just the white of the paper)*.

1. Draw the shapes you are going to use, not the detail you see.

2. I am going to paint in the background red. This is not tonal, just giving some colour. I have used

Size
36cm x 26cm
14" x 10"

MATERIALS/COLOURS USED
Arche Rough 90lb

French Ultra Marine

Burnt Umber

Alizarin Crimson

TONE

OUTSIDE
THE BAKER'S SHOP

Sometimes a composition can be enhanced by painting in tones only. Don't worry about colour or detail. Two great colours to use to achieve this are French Ultra Marine and Burnt Umber. Taking them through their full tonal range and using the cold of the blue and the hot of the Burnt Umber, you will be amazed at what it can achieve. You can end up with a very nostalgic style of picture that works really well.

1

1   Use Burnt Umber on its own and very watered down. Look for the warm very light shapes to paint. If you find it difficult to see the light shapes, squint at the reference material and look only for the very light areas. Do the same for the medium and then the dark. Don't make too much out of the detail.

2

3

2. Still using the Burnt Umber, mix slightly thicker, and add all the medium tones you can see.

I will use French Ultra Marine for the boy's jumper. His trousers can be a mix of the French Ultra Marine and the Burnt Umber.

3. Paint the medium-to-dark tones very quickly still using the SAA Whopper brush. Just take dollops of Burnt Umber and a dollop of French Ultra Marine and keep working through all the medium dark areas. The variation will break up the large areas of dark.

Size
54cm x 34cm
21" x 13"

One colour on its own would be tedious. Pick out the cakes and just paint quickly around the shapes that they make. You are painting the negative shapes.

The little dog is just a few blobs of light and dark shapes.

Finally, put in the lettering on the sign using Alizarin Crimson.

1

POOLE QUAY
ATMOSPHERE

MATERIALS/COLOURS USED
Fabriano Rough surfaced 90lb

Raw Sienna

Cadmium Yellow

Light Red

Cadmium Red

French Ultra Marine

Burnt Umber

Intense Violet

Cobalt Blue

Sepia

Prussian Blue

The atmosphere on Poole Quay is quite special, each evening can be quite different. Fireworks and live music one night, motorcycles or vintage cars another, the daytime being different again. The combination of the quaint old characterful pubs and warehouses, together with the relaxed holiday makers, creates an interesting atmospheric painting. Strolling along Poole Quay, you'll be amazed at what you'll find to inspire your painting.

2

Cadmium Red for the bright reds. Cadmium Yellow can be used for the other parasols.

4. I will paint the figures next as that will allow me to see how much detail I need to use on the buildings. The foreground figures are the focal point, so these need to be painted with stronger colours. I'll alter some of the colours of the clothes. You need to be aware that sometimes colours or tones are very similar to the background, and once painted can blend into the background.

1. I will draw this in a lot of detail. Using a Whopper brush, put on basic washes of colour. Mix a medium wash of Intense Violet for all the shadows on the buildings.

2. The red building can be Light Red. Mix a little Cobalt Blue to kill the brightness for the paving slabs. To give the impression of distance and recession, put a very pale wash of Cobalt Blue in the distance and then run the Light Red mix into that.

3. The bright parasols can be added using a pale wash of Intense Violet for the shadow area and

3

The more distant figures can be painted very loosely, using paler washes of French Ultra Marine Blue and Burnt Umber, with a few muted colours added.

5. Paint in the benches using Burnt Umber and a little French Ultra Marine Blue.

Now I can concentrate on painting the pub. I have used a mix of Sepia and Prussian Blue for the dark parts of the wood on the pub. Although in reality they are black, I don't

4

want the finished painting to look too oppressive.

Fill in any colours you can

see on the notice boards. Don't be too fussy with these, keep them loose and with very little detail. Use French Ultra Marine mixed with Burnt Umber for the window glass. Vary the tones slightly, and add a few different colours that you see. These need to be broken up. It looks very boring if you end up with every window exactly the same.

Fill any gaps with blobs and splashes of colour. French Ultra Marine mixed with Burnt Umber makes good English shadows.

5

Once the shadows are dry, use the end of a credit card with a little Sepia added to the edge to create the legs of tables and benches.

Finally, add some Cobalt Blue mixed with a little Light Red for the sky. I tend to paint the sky last, because once I have finished the rest of the painting, it then gives me an idea as to how dark or bright the sky can be to help the rest of the painting.

I decided that a 'cauliflower' which appeared at the very front of the painting didn't look very good, so I washed over it with some thick Raw Sienna. This helps to bring the foreground forward.

Size
34cm x 42cm
13" x 16"

1

WIMBORNE CRICKETERS

ATMOSPHERE

MATERIALS/COLOURS USED
SAA Whopper Brush
SAA Wash Brush
90lb Arch Rough Paper

Raw Sienna

Lemon Yellow

Cadmium Orange

French Ultra Marine
Blue

Burnt Umber

Intense Violet

Light Red

Sepia

Prussian Blue

Cricketers playing on a hot summer day conjure up nostalgic memories of traditional English summers spent watching families playing cricket on village greens. The players in their whites are perfect for picking out the shadows made by the sun, and create a very lively, three dimensional painting. You have a ready-made composition of movement and action. When you draw your players, focus on the light and dark shapes on the clothes, and just draw the shapes, not detail. I've drawn in the background house, as this is part of the scene that makes my painting Wimborne, but I've kept the house very 'loose', as I want the cricketers and their game to be the focal point.

1. Mix some Prussian Blue and some Lemon Yellow with lots of water. At the same time, make a watery mix of Raw Sienna. Using a Whopper Brush and the Raw Sienna, paint in the run and, whilst still damp, paint the surrounding area with the Prussian Blue and Lemon Yellow mix. I want to keep the green very translucent. Whilst still wet, add some almost neat Lemon Yellow to the right-hand corner,

2

figures to show up. There are only small bits of skin showing, and for these I've used Light Red with a hint of Sepia.

For the next figure, use a mix of French Ultra marine Blue with a very small amount

just to bring the foreground to the fore, and break it up slightly.

2. Paint the house very quickly and loosely; mix all your colours before-hand and paint very quickly. You want the colours to merge and blend. The viewer needs to be aware that there is a house in the background, but it's not a significant part of the composition. Although the window frames are white, they're very much in shadow. Using a wash brush, paint the white frames with a mix of Intense Violet and Burnt Umber. Whilst the frames are still damp mix some French Ultra Marine with Burnt Umber and paint all the brickwork. Also, add a little French Ultra Marine Blue to some of the windows.

3. Once dry, use a mix of Prussian Blue and Sepia for the darker panes of glass.

4. Make a mix of Prussian Blue and Lemon Yellow with quite a lot of water, and another mix of Prussian Blue and Sepia for the very dark English greens, work very quickly, letting the light and dark areas blend.

5. The white clothing is ideal for creating a truly three dimensional feel to the painting. For the shadows, I use Intense Violet for the majority of players, with a couple in French Ultra Marine Blue, just to add variety.

6. For the first figure, use Intense Violet mixed fairly strong. Don't be frightened of being too dark, you need some strong contrasts to allow the

3

4

5

6

of Burnt Umber added. This will separate the two figures. If you used the same shadow colours, you could end up with a strange figure that looked like it has two heads and four legs.

7. Work your way through all the figures, using mostly the Intense Violet, painting the very last figure in the French Ultra Marine Blue with Burnt Umber. Once the figures are completely dry, use a mix of Intense Violet and Sepia, with very little water, to create some dry brush marks for the creases in the clothes; keep this to a minimum. Some of the caps are painted with Cadmium Orange.

8. The stumps can be painted using the edge of a credit card and some Sepia. Rub the thick paint gently over the bumps on the surface of the paper.

9. The shadows are applied using Prussian Blue and Sepia, with a fair amount of water added. To balance the painting, I've put a large shadow across the right-hand side of the painting at the front. Know-one will know that there isn't a large building or tree causing it.

I think, that, by keeping this a long, thin, landscape composition, it adds interest to the scene. It gives it a lot more impact, and is slightly unusual.

8

9

7a

7b

Size
34cm x 42cm
13" x 16"

GALLERY

The Chase 25cm x 35.5cm

Bournemouth Busker

45cm x 35 cm

Street musicians make fantastic compositions for paintings. The energy and movement work so well. Sometimes, if you are lucky, you find the musicians are in sunshine, which, of course, never happens when they are on stage.

Eating Ice Creams, Weymouth

43cm x 33cm

This colourful back street in Weymouth is an absolute delight to paint. It has so much colour and a real 'holiday' feel to it. The figures eating ice cream just set the scene.

Ben at Weymouth
35cm x 45cm

This was one of the first paintings that I did. I used a photograph of my son in the sea. I decided to turn it into a water colour as a reminder of our holiday. My daughter later entered it into the SAA annual competition and I won the title of SAA Artist of the Year.

Horse & Cart Bruges
35cm x 45cm

This was a very cold November day, but the light in Bruges was brilliant. I have kept colour to a minimum and used the sun bleached pavements to add contrast to the composition.

Street Musicians
45cm x 28cm
These musicians were so energetic and full of energy, their brightly-coloured clothes also added interest to the painting.

The Dorset Hunt
45cm x 35cm
The movement of the horse and hounds on a hunt makes for interesting paintings. I sometimes alter the jackets to red, as this works well against the greenery.

Overleaf: The Great Dorset Steam Fair
46cm x 35cm
You can use any subject matter when you paint using tones. These figures concentrating on an old steam engine are a compelling subject.

By the same author:

Animals on the Loose.
(ISBN 978-09558088-0-7)
Features a variety of vibrant and colourful projects, each with step-by-step illustrations to help fire the imagination; this book and DVD set really is an *essential* for any artist who struggles to paint animals!

Book £12.99 • DVD £14.99
Available from:

The Studio Mill Lane Gallery,
9 Mill Lane, Wimborne
Dorset, BH21 1LN
Tel: 01202 880084
Mobile: 07789 026546

Index